Rue the Day

Tanis MacDonald

May 2012

Tanis MacDonald.

TURNSTONE PRESS

Turnstone Press
Artspace Building
018-100 Arthur Street
Winnipeg, MB
R3B 1H3 Canada
www.TurnstonePress.com

Turnstone Press gratefully acknowledges the assistance of the Canada Council for the Arts, the Manitoba Arts Council, the Government of Canada through the Book Publishing Industry Development Program, and the Government of Manitoba through the Department of Culture, Heritage and Tourism, Arts Branch, for our publishing activities.

Cover design: John Roscoe
Interior design: Sharon Caseburg
Printed and bound in Canada by Friesens for Turnstone Press.

Library and Archives Canada Cataloguing in Publication

MacDonald, Tanis, 1962–
    Rue the day / Tanis MacDonald.

Poems.
ISBN 978-0-88801-335-4

    I. Title.

PS8575.D6657R83 2008   C811'.54   C2008-900897-9

For all the smart girls who

Contents

Anchoress • 3

The Apprenticeship • 5
Smart Mouth • 13
Paper and Antimatter • 31
Litany in the Plague of Time • 45
Satellite of Love • 65
Banshee Hour • 81

Notes • 93
Acknowledgements • 95

Don't rue the day you were born,
But think of the poor, poor nightingale,
Who hadn't a sign of a thorn.

—A. Ethelwyn Wetherald

rue: sorrow; distress; repentance; regret.

a perennial evergreen shrub of the genus *Ruta*, esp. *Ruta graveolens*, having bitter, strong-scented leaves which were formerly much used for medicinal purposes.

to affect with penitence or contrition; to affect with sorrow; to distress; grieve.

to fall, decline.

Rue the Day

Anchoress

The woman in the cubic room will draw
her pointy knees up to her chin and fold
her arms into a knotted bow. Because
the room's too small, she'll bend to hold
her head against the lowering ceiling.
Her neck is arced, her spine a convex curve.
Her balance fine. Madame la Guillotine.
Her feet, too big for boots: her toes reserved
to flattened arches beneath her fetal weight.
The box she's in allows her oxygen
but little light. These hours past too late
for saving grace or plaintive cry and then
she shifts, not quite a shudder in the dark,
a drift of facial tics, a plangent smirk.

The Apprenticeship

the first and last thing you will

*

the smoky interior of her brain fools
            most people don't
               give up

                 she's been known to collapse
                     her bones into an easel
              she's been known to crash
                    a party at lightspeed
she'll fly off the handle
she'll take the leap
she'll move a mountain
she'll see too much say too little she'll

             use the wrong fork and lick the knife

                you'll never believe
                the paper she eats

    do not curse the length and breadth of her
              ego it's better to make the evil

      eye and spit when she crosses your path light
      a candle and draw a circle around anything she touches

you know her
women like her make
          women like me   .

she does not suffer

                        fools

*

she's a subject who speaks

and she's got all
     the answers when I call her
a muse she tosses
my eye against her fist when I call her
my fury she laughs

    revenge is a dish best broken

        her rotted flesh infinite rat's nest and summer tweed ragged
        mouth articulated legs with closed eyes she foresees all
        the usual deaths

    a woman needs a fury like a fish needs a river

she's the hand who grips the glass
        doorknob to the Underworld

     she patches my right eye and shoots the horse I rode in on
     she smiles with her cracked lips

    let's begin

her breath woodsmoke and skunk
     she shoves me through the door

    stay there until you learn

she apprentices me to her
she reverses Cassandra's curse

        I am always believed
        especially when I lie

*

she teaches me to read my own entrails
(a mean feat) she's pious and sneers
at haruspexes who take the auspices
like Victorians took the waters

don't be fooled by an exaltation of larks

she never casts bones or takes my
temperature she knows what I think
the moment she opens her mouth

and sighs

you're going to have to do better

or a lot worse

*

don't look now
she's got her hot
green eye on you

*

(the subject speaks)

*Listen. I can only tell you what I know
and it has nothing to do with the book or
the word and everything about the glow
of my head in the sun. Come closer. I will
tell you what you don't want to know.
It is neither more nor less terrible than
what you heard the last time you fell
so far you could not believe the bellow
when you landed. Enough. Hoick
yourself out of the pit. I will*

*tell you the first and last thing you will
never need to know. I will tell you a riddle
so you will believe, so you will fear
it is nothing. It has nothing to do. (I will
only say this once, so open your ears.)
The best riddle tells you.*

Smart Mouth

we think the world of you

*

Pert minx, little ticking time bomb,
I warned you of the day to come.
I told you that your eyes would steam,
your head crackle with static. Dumb
child, there's a price on your mouth. You
had to know, but you would not believe
until your left eye saw the angel suck
ink from the great book. Still you're naïve
enough that your sweet offerings amuse;
even the turnips you brought last time nod
their dumb mauve heads. They remind me
of you. Trust me. You're not sick or flawed
enough to be cured yet. Read what you wrote.
Sleep when you can. Make careful notes.

A Short History of the Back

Against the wall, upright on chairs, supine on beds, the back is settlement
and return, a way to silence, rest. Be warned of sudden pain, its syntax
of pops and yelps, a revolution in the lumbar region, extra vertebrae
trumpeting their right to curve the spine. Sciatica stings this column
of ivory, squeezes vortex into sculpture balanced on a twist. The
thoracic cavity leans on a tower of Babel and bone threaded through
the trunk. Walking upright is hazardous. It's the price of being taller
than orangutans in their monks' robes, moving in a straight line away
from the chimpanzee's amble, the gorilla's hump and heavy mastoid
process. Remember that day that our dorsal fin shrank down to muscle.
Trapezius. Intercostals. Back to back they faced each other.

& the brain (being the most erotic organ in the body
& the least appealed to)
After Rogal

the brain's a stunner.
it promises the body they'll make
beautiful museums together.

the brain's graduated cum laude in
making mountains from molehills.
the brain's a big liar but it's easily

fooled and so rarely appealed to
that it pants after every chance to prove
itself on a salacious field.

but the brain's a stickler. all
those peeler bars on Pembina Highway
have been newly renovated and every

man who passes by with me makes
a comment. do they expect
an expression of regret or interest

from me or from my brain
the most erotic organ in this or
any other body?

Birth of the Clinic

The body gave birth to the clinic on an overcast day in March. The body had hoped for a girl but the clinic was healthy enough. Two doors. Ten little windows. Striped mattresses. The efficient body swaddled the clinic and took it home. The oedipal body peeked into the clinic's linen closets and scribbled on all the charts but the clinic was colicky and shrieked unless held and walked. The exhausted body propped the clinic in front of reruns of *Marcus Welby* and the clinic gurgled and hummed with admissions. The clinic defecated pink pills. The yawning body changed the clinic's outpatient policy and tossed the soiled one in a pail of bleach and water. The clinic scowled and kicked. The body took everything. Sooner or later the clinic would boss the body. When the asylum was born, the sibling rivalry was fierce.

Patron Saint of the Misquoted

Weary we are, steeped in error and the gift
of double vision, exhaustion stitched to
our sleeves, a badge we earned with all those
late nights, good girl guides
of the semiotic. St. Ella, patron saint
of all who write stars far into the wee hours and
can't remember the point the next day: our lady
of misquotation understands our sacrifice
and smiles on us. When warned our faith is shallow
or misplaced, we can point to her lavender halo.
Our fatigue a holy sign: the curve of grey
skin beneath our eyes. The quick-witted pay
in the end, no smart mouth goes unpunished.

Job's Comforter

*Def. 1: the proverbial phrase for one who intends or professes to comfort, but does the opposite.**

Day 1
I can't imagine what you're going through.

Day 2
Think of it as good experience for next time.

Day 3
Well. It's not like you could take it with you.

Day 4
It could be worse.

Day 5
Look, everyone has problems.

Day 6
At least He notices you.

Day 7
You know, there's a book in this.

* 2. *(colloq.) a relentlessly cheerful bastard*

Advice to Young Poets

a poem ought to be
    fresh and simple

like an ironed gingham dress
    or a salad with grapefruit slices

or an ironed gingham dress with a single firm wrinkle ironed in by
the sweetly naïve and fresh-scrubbed girl who was simply
    distracted by
    a flaxen-haired child eating
    an apple rosy as the child's sexless cheeks

or a slightly wrinkled gingham dress with a few grass stains

or a gingham dress down which a salad with grapefruit slices has been
spilled, then ground in with the edge of the bowl

or a gingham dress flung off and stuffed in the back of the closet

a gingham dress that made the girl in it look like Grendel dressed as
Rebecca of Sunnybrook Farm

        (she was happy and why can't you be?)

In which the Writer looks into the Poem

This poem owns you, lifts you from
sleep, shakes you into your socks and down
in front. A real writer wouldn't take it, wouldn't

sit still for such bad treatment. No one likes
a know-it-all, and don't you know it.

The poem holds its hand over your mouth and
pinches your nostrils shut. You refuse the hood.
The poem's a sadist. It blows smoke in your face.

The poem insists it is worth more than the lines you count.
The poem claims it would be epic, if only.

The poem writes itself on your circadian
rhythms, salts your porridge, rides the humping
rails of peristalsis into your small intestine.

The poem is legion. You would thrust it into
the pigs but for their knowing eyes.

The poem is no angel, but you wrestle. The night is
eight stanzas long. Hip shanked into cadence:
impossible, necessary history.

In which the Poem looks into the Writer

Chaotic
fleshy entity.
Form inseparable
from content.
Rhythm?

In which the Writer wonders whether Auden was right

Poetry makes nothing happen over and over. Nothing
slides into your life and heaves itself onto your tall
lap. What a load of old bollocks. Nothing weighs
you down; you squeeze out from under and it lolls

at your feet, never shifts itself. Nothing's a lazy bastard.
Its great galumphing absence slows you. You trip
over its long naked tail on your way to the cellar,
where you want to hide from the nothing ripped

from poetry. Spiders spin webs between your fingers.
Arachnids know from nothing. So does damp.
Something shuffles from behind the box of books
you saved from the fire, curling adventures and camp

manuals, something small shambles out. It's
nearsighted and does not love your excuses.
Something's ugly and nothing's got the long
sick suck of shallow good looks. It's got its uses.

It burns the fat of time in heat units of revision.
Your undivided attention. Nothing's your decision.

In which the Writer gets advice during speech therapy

Once you get the hang of it, believe
me, it's not so hard. Not so much like
dying as you may believe. Take
a breath into your lungs, though it burns
with the high hot ting of oxygen. Drop
your lower jaw for the first syllable. Widen
your mouth for the vowel, the one that refers
to you, yourself, the active subject. Now
press your lips together as though you're
deep in thought and hum. This will
contract the verb into the subject; mash
them together. No need to stand
on ceremony. Now the hard part; only
the few and brave dare go this far. Begin
with a hiss. Don't linger on the serpent's
tongue; leap to the sound you'd make
in sympathy if a child fell off a bike,
not hurt, but with a bruised sense of
failure that comes from trying too hard,
or not at all. You'll like the next bit; growl
as though you were only a little afraid.
Then, at last, grin like you mean it.
Show your teeth and pronounce
the most common vowel in our language.
Now you're home free. Try it all together
with me once. I'm sorry. Again, I'm sorry.

In which the Writer reads

If I wasn't watching the sky, I would write off any horizon.

If I hadn't read this line in John Newlove's book, I wouldn't be writing.

If I hadn't hauled out my bike and ridden eight kilometres to the library to get out Newlove's book, I wouldn't be writing.

If I hadn't worked in a branch library for five years, I wouldn't have found Newlove's misshelved book, and I wouldn't be writing.

If all the undergraduates hadn't gone home to their small towns, if they hung around the library all summer, smoking cigarettes and borrowing all the Newlove, I wouldn't be writing.

Energy equals mass times the velocity of light squared. Relativity notwithstanding, this has nothing to do with writing. Newlove says.

Work Habits

I am up with the dawn, gurgling with ideas.
I rise with the chickens, and scribble down their scratches.
I fall out of bed, and doodle until something better comes along.

I research all my ideas before beginning a thoughtful first draft.
I read until my eyes bleed.
I mention my idea over lunch and blot it with a napkin.

I proofread assiduously for spelling errors and logical inaccuracies.
I proofread in terror of the looming margin of error.
I proofread for the laughs, and correct nothing.

I am happy to consult with my colleagues about their work.
I never leave the house or answer the phone.
I keep my brain in a water glass.

The light shines through it.

A Poet Ticks

You know she does. She ticks like a stopwatch timing the fastest
sentence in the west, speech act after speech act, and what's her
perlocution?

She ticks like a bomb, but she's not the bomb, she's just one more
writer with one more bag of tricks, or bag of ticks, a whole burlap sack
teeming with wood ticks and potato bugs, insects of punctuation and
drag, oh someone fumigate her house, someone take a hot needle and
lance the tick fattening on her O positive.

She ticks like a lead pencil following a list, checking off item by item,
making sure everything's in its place until the list dissolves into a mush
of paper left out in the rain beside the red wheelbarrow, the manuscript
pecked at by those damn white chickens.

She ticks like an egg timer, like a woman pacing in kitten heels
succumbing to a variety of facial and bodily tics, tiny seizures of the
arm or neck. She's ticked off and not going to take it anymore: a tisket,
a tasket, hands off that blown gasket. She's got her ticket to ride, she's
got her walking papers, she's taking her own tick, talking it up right, and
who's going to tell her that she's not?

Eumenides (The kindly ones)

We think the world of you
and if it wasn't for your blank face or
your strange walk, for that ill-chosen
phrase, for your flip questions and
clever comments, you'd be our dream
girl and we'd keep you with us forever but
as it is, we need you to
understand nothing

we say has anything to do with
you. When we say

No *and* get out *and* over your dead body *we say it*
with love, all things being equal, in the best
interests of all concerned. We say it with all due
respect and every good intention, we speak for
your own good, we speak secure
in the knowledge

you are smart enough to know better. Now don't
disappoint us.

Paper and Antimatter

who let you out to do the wishing?

Warning

What can I say about chewed
nails or ragged quicks, my arms
and the man inside them? What
left undone, who left uncharmed?

(Pipecleaner-thin arms in puffed
sleeves at the wedding up north;
when we danced, my father warned me
not to lead. What's memory worth?)

Behind crossed arms, I watch a woman
stand tall in her kitchen; she insists
people can be broken like toys. I bite
down to the quick; the dead persist.

The Heart Fails

to move ahead, stalls and can't always draw on the reserve, the heart
wants and goes silent, goes quickly with a woman on her knees trying
to kick-start it, a woman by the bed checking the chart, a woman in
the kitchen baking tarts. The heart fails even as it reaches; it is only a
hollow organ. Auricle, ventricle: the heart tries but can't make it to the
next breath. The heart fails to remember the foolish talk or bad faith,
the arguments and cracked crockery. The heart keeps its own counsel in
the fibrous sac of the pericardium. The heart fails as a perpetual motion
machine; it fails as a ledger. Read the heart's silence as a sentence with
impossible grammar, as the variable in a formula whose value cannot
always be determined. Heart = x. Heart = colourless green idea,
sleeping furiously.

Caesura

Since my father seized
with the nurse at his
elbow, the horizon crowds
a dull mourning. Forecast:
molasses, winter, night, day

a screech across a blackboard. Good
advice to be on time in clean clothes
is enough to keep me prostrate and
filthy. Water is a glass of sleep.
Pour it on petulant skin.

Skating Lesson

The body wears out with motion, a sway,
exposure to the air. Entropy sounds
a silent bugle. Time will shear away
these walls and ceilings painted brown.

A point of reckoning, the family counting
house closed and now abolished.
Stones silent on the porch, a mounting
quiet in the kitchen, dining table polished

like a pond. Lace your skates and push out
onto the ice. Trust it to take your weight
balanced on that thin strip of metal. Flout
the veneer. Carve onto its face a figure eight,

the curves of a circle, sudden stop. Let
the wind into the house to freeze
your cheeks, let it gust against
the drawn blue curtains, watch it tease

the end of your bound hair in vast
chilling sweeps, let your scarf sag
with ice pellets from your breath. One last
lesson: wet wool, aching legs, ashes in a bag.

Signature

The week he died the cold raked
me no matter how many cups of tea
I gripped. That week I bore the weight
of detail and absence, a forward ache,
paper and antimatter. I forgot how
to follow the frostline of words into
a sentence, into plot and complication,
to the final turn of a phrase or a vow.
That week with my pen I tendered
my signature on papers that sent him
where he was already gone, I cooked
and did not eat. I found a needle to mend
his wool socks. A chance to extend
the life of the foot. World, end, amen.

Eulogy

But they that wait upon the Lord shall renew their strength; they shall mount up with wings as eagles; they shall run, and not be weary; and they shall walk, and not faint.

—Isaiah 40:31

They shall eat blue cheese and mow the lawn as often as they like; they shall play slow-pitch and lawn bowl every weekend; they wash the car repeatedly and slip a leash around the neck of the neighbour's dog to take her on long secret walks. They shall eat buns. They shall go to the opera and have good seats; *Nabucco* or *Tales of Hoffmann* will play. They shall visit the Agricultural Fair and smell the heavy horses; they shall attend bonspiels and tell of the 1943 championship. They shall pour the angel's dram and discuss the smoothness of whiskey, its peaty quality. They shall walk and walk and not feel the earth shift beneath their feet, they shall take easy air into their lungs, they shall be straight of back and great of heart, they shall beat their old batting average, they shall not fall, nor stir, nor stumble; they shall rise and move forward like workmen or philosophers, they shall not faint.

Little

Before I leave, I remove my black glove
and reach to shake the hand of the funeral
director. He is young and nervous of love;
I pause, assure him, this occasion viral.
The death certificate displays an error—
wait, two—and there's no way I'll let
my father's final document go out blurred,
misspelled, a first forgetful draft. Forget
grief; I make it right. I lift my father high
with my inky hands. I am tall, almost Amazon,
perhaps proportionate but never small. I
think of my little father, thin even on
ice cream, and shorter than me for so long.

The box that holds his ashes heavy as stone,
as though decision massed to compact
the flesh and grew in size. In a cloth sack:
a last velvet overcoat. The size exact
to fit my arm's bent crook: he's snug against
my sleeve, he swings inside my elbow's bone
hammock, rocked between ulna and humerus.
We walk into November. A winter day:
the sky slips low. The car. Suburban house.
I hold him up to see the rutted ice, the snow
and slush, the lights on twiglets. Without delay,
I count degrees in Celsius: he'd want to know.

I hold my father up to the car's clouded dome
of light. It's true, I tell him, we are almost home.

Take Measure

What spills out of us, what spills over
into the dragtown of bitterness, gall.
Catch it in a cup. Measure the meniscus.

The trees too brown, every shade of green
withered. Who let you out to do the wishing?
Inmates run the asylum; hear them praying

for rain. Long lines lead on, the highway
stutters into the horizon. Days fake their own
despair; dissolution hides in a book

or behind the drama of death. What foolish
pursuits. Hand me the antidote; I'm sick
of the road home. Bring me to the tuba, its

deep sad notes, the player's puffed cheeks, music
like soft shouting, or a wise moan, a whale
in pain, an elephant kneeling in its graveyard.

The curve of the liquid at the lip of the cup.

Elegy without Water

not even a year and already there are too many
dead fathers reaching up from their couches

and easy chairs to be missed in photos and at
tables and who knows how long my dead father

       will keep saying he would have loved it if he

caught the steam train with us to the sweet dust
sawmill that one day we took off up the Malahat

my father would have talked a blue
streak to the porter with the one green eye

       grinned his denture grin at the double saws

shaken his head at the film we shot of
the singing blacksmith with his clean

apron and swept forge and the weasel who darted
into the bush at the whir of the camera all

       things my father would have loved if

Confession

Damn. The bird on the branch is too
red to be living, too swift in its flight
across the square, too bright for you.
A warning. These clouds are not right,
apocalypse without despair. Sinned
against is sinning. The elegy lies.
No amount of water. This little hand.
My father resembled my father. Spies.
I have done it. The king of cups
did not reassemble my father. 'Tis pity
you are learned, and not a whore, or witty
without those florid hips. The bird flies up
like blood to stain the sky and I
earned my seat by his left hand, first
remembrance, last to know. Try
to test me on this morning after the frost,
your long white hair plucked and woven
into a cuckoo's nest. How will you last?

Daylight: Saving

Elongated winter into spring, frail
white months splinter into slivers
and then the scent of mud. Last year's

deaths march me into the sun. Too pale
by half: I'm nearly blue. The window
box ekes out tight mauve buds. Let me

weigh in on this one: photosynthesis
expects so much. Mid-month approaches
with its anniversary of birth, its killing

Ides. Out, damned spot, like a lion. A snap
in the synaptic weave. I grow older, that slow
virus, predictable as hunger or sleep,

rain or a deadline, words that will not
line up, mucks in a row. Once again.
Winter, sun, march, window, long, birth,

death. Finches in the cedar nest too close to
the cat's mouth. Again. White spring, mud,
soapbox of grief, mourning's long and gritty

residence. Rattled sleep. Death, nest, mouth.
The virus in the mauve rain. Anniverse.

*

*Tell me. I won't promise to listen, or even remember
the thing you thought would never happen. I'm
a plague: I'll catch you. Or I'll walk away or laugh
when you speak. Necessity tells tales about crimes
you've not committed, the one thing no one has ever
understood about you, or what you might do if
you let yourself: the rock, the cypress by the river.
I can see the fire, the small eyes of animals spying.
Come on. There's no statute of limitations on lying.*

Litany in the Plague of Time

let me let trouble

(the old deaths come back

*

Oh, it's not over. You should consider
yourself under arrest. Consider yourself primed.
Prepare to debate the law or better yet, its
miscarriage. Kick out against it before time

rears up on its hind legs: too late. See
yourself boxed in, kept on ice, left to rot,
in stir. It's a long apprenticeship to sitting,
a pool of space, a blur of silence. You thought

you could crush time into a capsule you could
swallow, ingest? Fear coats your gums with grit.
Slow your metabolism. Wrest entropy from its spot
napping on the calendar. How will you strap it

to the room's pendulum? What spins the bed?
Sit up and meet vertigo, the swing in your head.

*

the old deaths come back on their own hitch
        whir in your head   a caesura
    a spanner in your works

cruel as a clock the season   sashays up the sidewalk
    flares its nostrils

        and lisps seven cursed syllables in a child's high whisper
    season of dog days and no good
                reason
                  borrow what you can steal
      beg an eye to recall   the colour of distance

                        blue

Tennessee knew

all about the old deaths
        how they come back

how they say they want

      nothing from you

*

Trouble is   Trouble never

                                  ends

        she wiles away the time
                patient as the grave

strings the day out to   the thinnest strand
        Trouble waits for you
            to lift her into your lap   even if you pretend you can't
        see her spinning in the corner of your eye

        Trouble invented lip-synch   she knows how to mouth the
words   she dressed the devil in drag and wrote the tune

and you

                        can't call shots
                          you can't see

        the trouble with Trouble
is the attention she craves
            the time she takes
                Trouble doesn't know how to do without

so she fills your head with static

let me remind you
let me blind you
let me let Trouble into your life

you'll know her by her long listening ears

*

what plagues us
    what snaps our heads to
rights and won't let us look
    at look over look alive

    what swarms us

and collapses each cliff we climb
    stretches a long wide mouth
into a smile into a yawn
    into the abyss that looks

    into you

tearing up the floorboards
    as mosquitoes buzz
logarithms in your blistered ear
    and frogs teach empty bottles

    how to croak

you can only cover the hole with a tarp
    like a trap in a cartoon
you can only remember so long
    to step around it

    this is how

you flirt with disaster

*

she has a permanent contempt for
     cars and people who drive them but
she demands you pick her up and
     sinks her sharp teeth into your shoulder
if you don't floor it the moment she shuts
     the door and opens her mouth

You look like you've lived the good life.
Nothing always happens, mile after mile,
to you. I'll bet you keep all your hair
in a box in case it comes back in style.

*

shake a martini with a single
ice cube frozen from the waters of Lethe

    when you meet him Jesus turns out to be
    the kind of guy who wears a T-shirt on a date

    who says *it's not you it's me*
    who you think of not as the one

    who got away but as the one who
    waited for half an hour

    before he confessed all
    you knew just by looking

forget the olive
bruise the gin

*

in the morning you run like chaos is the time you have to beat

count the houses you pass

how many new porches
how many painted this year by girls you knew
how many did you step inside
and wait for her to paint herself ready

run by the house of the boy who believed
in female divinity that hot July
and by the ruins of the house of the girl who believed

she was John the Baptist   ate locusts for breakfast and hated
you

you should have kept your big mouth   shut
when he married the angel of the house   and she died
when she signed the order for demolition   and vomited stars

but the eyes of the quiet houses make you grandiose
enough to think saying nothing is best

besides locusts make good eating
covered with chocolate

the dark so good for your heart

*

that conclusive winter pitched
        notes you could not reach over the waterfall of books

          surging over the sluice gate until apprentices and scribes
              were swept over the falls because they always did
          as the furies said   and were never heard from again

except for you when you bobbed up in the wake   flotsam
        (o how knowledge rained   like needles)

damn you then to the making of books   there is no end
the pained lustful slap of phonemes   language's outstretched toe
will trip you and study is a weariness of the flesh

        (o the mistakes you made   instead of pages)

ghosts will proofread while you sleep
the bloody-minded trip-loaded sleep of a Jonah

beneath the glaucous green eyes of the woman who
promised you grief   who knew
what ink would do   who could foresee

           what has already passed

*

a year later you wake up
with three damp sentences balled in your fist

patina of dust listening in the next room
(bad housekeeping bad religion)

hearing charm drain out of you like pus
when you hook these words into

the wall and climb them until
the combined weight of tin and paper

brings you crashing

*

late at night
you google the dead
of course they are not

           there (what is absence in cyberspace)
           only traces

of the name it's a trick to find them
where they are not   (what is sleight of hand in mourning)

but sometimes when you try a different search
engine be damned if he's not gone

on to a career in kinesthesiology
at an American university

maybe an afterlife's relative who can say

the man living with his name does
not know his own chances   (what is a run of luck in the plague of time)

*

you're penitent without sinning in the afternoon and you
        scrub the kitchen floor to the crawling
whir of a mower slicing the lawn down to a measured half inch
        while you drink your dogged weight in water

        the body's capacity for error is too large
you would like to envy (if it weren't a sin) the grass its sedentary life

last night on your keyboard you woke
        the dead who now wander past your house
so at dusk you must bake a lone potato
        and leave it beneath a pat of butter on the porch
for the nostrils of hungry ghosts for your sins of omission

        trouble is your ghosts don't

drift through walls or plot revenge but sit humped
        at the kitchen table and never come out with it
like chemists or cartographers
        working on a problem they can't talk for fear of

        ruining the design

don't ask the living are so crass
        with our curiosity and all our talk about nothing

*

the angel of history has sharp teeth
it flies backward in a hot wind
its paper-thin skirt over compass legs
its eyes slip

    time dents the angel of history
    but we insist on narrative even when

it has to stop and wake the dead this angel clutches
to its sternum of scrolls she collects
books written in storerooms

    burned banned banal the angel can't
    read

the cranes of its origami fingers sigh
flip pages
material

    progress

*

You don't fool me, minx. Grief has its uses.
Everyone learns to mourn. Everyone loses.

But you are apprenticed to me.
I expect more from a future fury.

Some mourn by cold, and some by fire; some on the page,
some with metal and wire; some mock, some rage.

Open your left eye, rub it with rue.
You'll see there what's next to do.

*

the gift is a poison
I can't swallow

bile hardens and vitriol
spits back cruel

women and men take it out
on each other

take it out like garbage

cited:

one hothead
fierce as frost

one cold bitch
who won't flinch

*

How could you think?
Of course I might

and more—I'll be quiet
if you're right.

*

let me trouble you let me
        listen to the sound beneath your voice knocking
against my head

I'm sorry it's come to this but

sincerity is so fake
        especially when you really mean it
it's a good thing you know what you're doing
it's a good thing the angel of revision
        loaned you his smashed harp

whoever's skin you've slipped on today
whatever's rotting in the visible universe

let me remind you the mixing of matter and
        antimatter results in the annihilation of both
you are not a conundrum of particle physics but

        an undefined article
        a floating pronoun
        not particularly personal

let me remind you that penitence is perhaps
outdated but not dead

put down those scissors
if no one tells you what to do   ,
                allow me

                to read you

*

the riot act:
        do not reply

rue the day I
        do not fall or fly

steering Necessity
        is not for the weak

the dubious lesson:
        love takes cheek

Satellite of Love

when I get my hands on you

Matrimony

*…women are the biggest single bad thing Zeus
has made for us; a ball-and-chain; we can't get loose*
—"An Essay on Women," Semónides of Amórgos

i. The Mud Wife

A green thumb for certain, though
a poor hand with a broom. She limps
when it rains, and fears the fire in
the grate. Serves salad for breakfast.
Knows nothing bad, and suspects
good is verdant but she doesn't own
the language to speak it. Her family
is quiet, though her brother wakes
every thousand years and wreaks
havoc at the borders of town. Her
children are always grubby, though
they'll pick berries all day and laugh
at thorns. She's cloddish but will
never leave you. You love her tickle
in your ribs late at night, her grit
between your teeth.

ii. The Weasel Wife

Your best cufflinks go missing. You
don't care. The shiny stream you pour
from your pocket at the end of the day,
silver she stirs into the air. Her whipcord
spine bends to listen at doors. But for the first
time in years, you balance each month. She
cooks stew and polishes silverware, while
the root cellar grows pyramids of parsnips
and paper. She reads everything. She keeps
her figure: you can't complain. She's
a brown reed of a woman who slips into
the room where she keeps accounts,
rolling a nest of bills into a coffee can.

iii. The Monkey Wife

Smart as paint, she's good with tools and not
afraid of climbing up to shingle the roof. Fresh
fruit every day, great for the kids. She's sweet-
tempered, ready to grin with those big beautiful
teeth. She loves a party, and it shows. She winds
her arms around your neck and kisses by the book.
She can't swim and screams when the dog runs by.
It's so damn ugly, she says, *and it smells like
death.* She hates it when you shave. She works
in a lab, looks better in her long white coat than
in any dress. You fell in love with her hands
around the test tube held up to the light, her
curious look, *eureka* in her eyes.

The History of Sexuality

starts somewhere with music
and your gender
of choice wearing skin over tendon

progresses to a profile
that drops your jaw

leads to walking
across the room (smokysilent
crowdedhot)

leads to dancing

leads to a room with someone who
looks like or smells like or sounds like
someone you are sure knows you
from somewhere and

finishes a conversation you never began

moves to a smaller room
with wine or coffee
whiskey or beer or oxygen

leads to wondering about
love on a cellular level

ends with small talk
sweat and a skewed angle

starts with the night the day
the meal you skipped the letter you could
not find one that would tell you

of the lime-pulp of Eros
the long cool fingers of Aphrodite

the promise of

Possibilities

The first room we share has a window
facing west that swallows the coin of
the sun. The antenna atop the next roof
casts a thin lizard's shadow over us
every winter afternoon. Chimera,
satellite of love. Those long February
days strange women ask after you, and I
hammer our story into shape. Everything's
one more guess in the dark. I pull you down
around my ears like a hat. The women
lurk on the fire escape, materialize behind
books on the library shelf, warn me
these things don't always work out. We
shoot a game of pool around a woman in
a trench coat who checks your pockets
for quarters. What did you do that they
service you with such envy? They all want
to know who I am, but cut their eyes when
I say: I come from the east, I am
the juggler of oranges and knives, I
the red-handed harlequin, the leopard
with stripes, the queen of taut
tripwire. You are my best nightmare, my
impossible plot. Rumour runs off
at the mouth, but knowledge is overrated.
Each night falls unlike the last; I don't know
what I'll do when I get my hands on you.

Scar Science
After Ondaatje

A boy with whom I sat stirring
at a lab table balanced a scar
that crawled the length of his left arm,

radius embraced by the static legs of
a centipede while he and I measured salt
grain by grain into the beaker until

the solution changed to saturate. Salt
thickened into snow, a build-up of cells,
like scar tissue, the lowly

worm on his arm recording data
and hypothesis, our method, the conclusion
we could not predict until we saw it form,

like the slice bisecting your eyebrow
where no hair will grow after the downhill flight
that landed you on your skull. You recall

the concussed crack that scared your rescuers,
who were sure you had knocked yourself
brainless. The scar red as a misplaced comma

above your eye when we argue about words or
other surprises. Meet me now in the kitchen
to measure all that accumulates between us,

the saturate of our life together, to watch the way our
heads break open, and the worm beneath
the skin rises to the surface.

Facts and Further Arguments

In retrospect, the gossip was right. I was
long in the tooth for first love, but time is
rough and I rode hard, put it away
wet. Unpacking the kitchen
one more time as you wire the new lights,
this time in a house we bought on faith
and the courage summoned from
serendipity, I have to laugh so I won't
scream. Time is not our friend. The deer
by the river was nothing like the moose
we saw struck and kicking on the shoulder.
One more city and a steep learning curve.
Too much revelation can bring a girl down.
A phalanx of bankers and lawyers said
too much about material
conditions, the way we live now.
To say I miss our years with nothing
would be untrue, but I miss the way you
made the smallest of rooms into a submarine,
a place for everything, Rube Goldberg rococo,
the way you made love out of breath, and
the way you spread a kindly layer on my spiky
life, made me look up at the spreading sky
and guess there was a future I hadn't yet seen.

Aubade

You don't want to know today's
date, but the sun's woken you.
Suffice to say it's late; the cat
laughs, and your hand's cramped
into a hook. Our snarled sheets
wage war, make lists, sloth.
Welcome to our usual bed.
There's no house martinet to
note our lack of hospital corners,
the sock between in the sheets.
We await the arrival of someone who
maintains a standard of cleanliness
to which we would like to become
accustomed. Rain falls, icicles
form, tragedy wears wet shoes.
Some days I could fall asleep on my
hips, dull as a Clydesdale. Theories
of incompleteness may be worth our
effort, but they clarify nothing. Still
we make our way; we make
our bed and lie about ways
we can recall the beauty of order.
The train we can see from the window
brings its boxcar logic into our green
room, a piece of prairie in this hot valley.
The engine whistles the city down
into pieces we can parse like sentences:
subject, object, the unfinished phrase
of us as we are this year on old sheets
with no fire escape, in the bed we
bought that day the car broke down
and we needed some place to rest
our buzzing heads.

Promise to the House

After Scofield

Let me take you in my arms, old house
with your wheezing walls and good
bones so strong in the high winds,
walls scribbled on by generations
not my own. Harold was here, and Joan, and
now the two of us, with our familiars of fur
and ink. Old house, you ragged diva of brick,
plaster, dried wallpaper paste, I have heard
you weep at night, and know you long
for people to ring your doorbell, to walk your
floors, to swing limbs and sleep smiling in
your rooms. You have seen sorrow, I know,
and a little madness. But let me tell you, large

soul of the house, sweet lonely house, when
I was ushered into your huge heart with my head
on fire, I knew you. I will not hear a word
against you. I know what you need, faith in
attention and muscle, strokes with sponge and
brush, an embrace of wood, sheetrock, a lick of
paint, spectacle made over and over in the soft
light of plaster dust. Old woman, we'll sand you
smooth. We'll measure you for robes of verdant
green with the tang of raspberry. Let us take you

into our future, house with a tiny kitchen, eccentric of
the block, crone who has seen so much, dowager
empress with your brick skirts and hibiscus
shoes, Miss Havisham without a wedding cake,
old widow, old maid, grandmother of invention, let us
cool you, clean you, fill you with the scent
of cardamom and rising yeast. We will show you
our mettle. When you get to know us, you will find
we are not afraid of hard work, or of love.

Labour Day

I read the last version of creation I'll read
before the term begins, I read the world's
firmament and ground, the metamorphosis,
chaos into order when you walk in with

the photo of our last city: the night balcony
with a sickle moon and star, the Turkish flag
emerging from the cherry trees in blossom.
We mocked all talk of Eden, lived mapless.

Oh that mouth of yours. I thought love was
a road sign I could scout out, then turn or not,
as I chose. I thought I knew how to drive. Love
lifts its gorgon's head and turns me to flesh.

The cat grows thinner and more vocal; the tumour
presses on her thyroid. You build shelves for my
books, the router growling in the basement. I could
lay a safe bet on your odd habits, but it's gone

six o'clock; the creation of the world's done for
the day. I'm a chatelaine rattling a ring of keys,
a suffragette in a new city under the same moon.
I will spend months talking about transformation,

the changes we make and remake. Tonight I stain
the new shelves, three coats; the fumes rise
in waves to stun the part of my brain that learned
to talk about logic and geography. Paradise.

Convergence

Elementary as a periodic table,
    aligning the planets is someone else's
version of magic. We cannot

    bray at the book of lies as we
write it. This stillpoint a maelstrom.
    A head turns the best of us

into Philistines. The prophet with ragged
    nails chews the trust cake we baked
by hook or crook in the cellar ovens.

    Keep the man who claims your red
silk and the woman who sings
    your song in the labyrinth. The past

is product. We met in a year of
    Wednesdays, as the blue moon broke
into even pieces, and an old story of ships

    and swords fell at our feet, called us
mages, divine. Charlatans, we
    gave it away. Fools, we saved

what we could. Icicles on the eaves.
    Fire in winter. We learned to choose.

*

Some trick, minx.

Your silent
Sphinx.

Banshee Hour

I.

This winter the myths
have taken a sabbatical.

February is a brisk caesura:
the wind a hyperbolic whip.

The truth used to trail
me like a bloodhound.

(Let no day pass without
discussing goodness or ghosts.)

I lost my wits on a rainy
northern road beside a grey goose.

In the war on logic, I
have dug my own trench.

II.

By March, I'll sing the crone's song.
No question, no answer.

Still forget to count, add, spell
out the calendar.

I thought poems would last
forever—I was wrong.

This year the furnace claims pride
of place. The bricks stay silent.

The frigid floor conspires against all
cadence. The road to my house cracks.

The river's pressure ridge and open
water. The sun a stark surprise.

III.

We rattle in the space we
never expected to furnish.

There is room here for
more than our good ideas.

If I blink too slowly, you vanish
into the labyrinth of rooms.

Who knows when you'll find your
way out and what you'll do then?

Will you materialize when I spin
a thread from my hair?

I'll fling it down the open drain
in the place we landed.

IV.

In our first apartment, she
dropped in without notice.

She heard my fingers striking keys
and bared her banshee teeth.

She held our bliss beneath a magnifying
glass and asked all those questions.

Old friends found you watching
my mind in full possession.

How silent I was the year I learned
about death and taxes.

I knew the body's failure to thrive
was her touch.

V.

Books come and go. We
read, return, discard.

Ink withers. Paper tears.
Movers charge by the pound.

I cannot say this thing I have
arrived on the page to speak.

I will use the second best words
in the second best order.

Cohabitation is for the birds:
swans, geese, eagles, owls.

What does it take to feather a nest?
Sheets, pillows, rag ends of towels.

VI.

Now it's the banshee hour. I am awake.
Three hours' sleep is a hard slap.

I watch you snore, spread like an x marking
the spot in a treasure hunt.

The house hums. Money shrieks out the windows.
Best just to practise the habit.

Words and names: what signifies?
Make sense like snow drifts.

Some will furrow their brows. Some will
claim it's not enough, and they will be right.

You sleep the sleep of the stern.
I am not a camera.

VII.

They say it's never too late but
the effort wipes me out.

Every day I find love
is not for the bloody-minded.

I wanted to run but the ends
of the earth were too far.

My paranoia leaves me checking
at borders for contraband.

I've combed desire into the quilt.
Did I tell you?

There are seven forbidden words
and now I've said two.

VIII.

Our tenth anniversary whistles
like a train in the night.

Wonder if we'll hop it. Wonder
if the hoboes in us would love it.

A decade. Feature it.
Deck. Aid. Dess. A mate.

Everyone wonders if you are some
kind of mirage. I'm not insulted.

I know you are. You play speed
metal in the kitchen.

Ten years since I cooked
an egg.

IX.

Same ten since I hung
a picture.

The hardware store:
necessity and nightmare.

The washing machine
a cobra. Bite back the scream.

Being single used to be
a problem. Being single used.

Poems undo their own rows.
Filigree and finish. Stop it.

No. Stop it
right now.

X.

Can you promise to cool
my forehead as it revs?

You are the only one who
reminds me of you.

Let down the chair from the ceiling,
though the pulley shrieks in protest.

You've outsmarted the squirrels
at last: thieves, devourers.

Not long ago, I thought
the next minute would dissolve.

What have you done to me lately.
Score: one hot jolt. Is my face red.

Notes

My thanks to the many writers and artists whose work ghosts these poems: Plato, Homer, Ovid, Christopher Fry, William Shakespeare, Thomas Nashe, John Milton, authors and translators of the King James Bible, Samuel Taylor Coleridge, Kurt Gödel, Emily Dickinson, Oscar Wilde, Coventry Patmore, Walter Benjamin, Virginia Woolf, Paul Klee, Ludwig Wittgenstein, Noam Chomsky, Michel Foucault, Jacques Derrida, W.H. Auden, William Carlos Williams, Tennessee Williams, Emily Carr, Christopher Isherwood, Rod Serling, Pierre Boulle, Raymond Carver, Lou Reed, Michael Ondaatje, Robert Priest, John Newlove, Jay Macpherson, Erin Mouré, Anne Carson, Andrea Martin, Catherine O'Hara, and Ken Garnhum.

"That conclusive winter" works with Ecclesiastes 12:12-13: "Of making many books there is no end; and much study is a weariness of the flesh. Let us hear the conclusion of the whole matter."

The title of "& the brain (being the most erotic organ in the body & the least appealed to)" is from "The Haunt Transformation: 4" in Stan Rogal's *(sub rosa)* (Wolsak and Wynn, 2003).

"Promise to the House" is after "Prayer for the House (we are leaving)" in Gregory Scofield's *Singing Home the Bones* (Polestar, 2005). My thanks to Greg for the conversation that led to this poem.

"Scar Science" is after "The Time Around Scars" in Michael Ondaatje's *There's A Trick With a Knife I'm Learning to Do* (McClelland and Stewart, 1979).

The primary definition of "Job's comforter" and all the definitions of "rue" come from *The Oxford English Dictionary*.

The excerpt from A. Ethelwyn Wetherald's "The Nightingale and the Thorn" appears in *Lyrics and Sonnets* (1931).

Acknowledgements

For their conversation, recommendations, and useful friction throughout the years that I worked on this book, I thank: Karen Clavelle for telling me about Poetry 365; Mavis Reimer, Smaro Kamboureli, Misao Dean, Keith Louise Fulton, Neil Besner, and Catherine Hunter for keeping watch over me at various times; Deborah Schnitzer for showing me Klee's *Angelus Novus*; Ryan Land for serving as poetry's greatest ambassador; John Barton for reminding me what poetry does; and John Roscoe for the final two lines of "Possibilities," and for everything else.

Thanks are also due to all my colleagues, students, and writer friends in British Columbia, Manitoba, and Ontario, for listening as I talked about and around these poems.

This book would not have been produced without the hard work and casual heroism of those who labour at the wheel of Turnstone Press. They keep poetry alive in Canada and accomplish numerous spectacular feats before breakfast without breathing hard. Special thanks must go to my editor, Sharon Caseburg, for making thoughtful demands of this book and for risking the wrath of the Fury.

Some of these poems first appeared on the *Studio* website maintained by the University of British Columbia's Faculty of Education. Thanks to Rishma Dunlop for arranging this. Earlier versions of some of these poems have been previously published in *Contemporary Verse 2, Event, Prairie Fire, PRISM International, The Malahat Review,* and *The New Quarterly,* and in the anthology *A/Cross Sections: New Manitoba Writing.* My thanks to the readers and editors of these publications.